NAME: Justine

BIRTHDAY: December 14

FAVORITE ANIMAL: Butterfly

FAVORITE COLOR: Pink with sparkles

FUN FACT: Justine loves writing poems!

NAME: Emme

BIRTHDAY: March 6

FAVORITE ANIMAL: Giraffe

FAVORITE COLOR: Dark Blue

FUN FACT: Emme's an aunt

NAME: Matt

BIRTHDAY: May 24

FAVORITE ANIMAL: Dog

FAVORITE COLOR: Blue

FUN FACT: Matt is an amazing artist

NAME: Toby

BIRTHDAY: July 28

FAVORITE ANIMAL: Dogs

FAVORITE COLOR: Blue

FUN FACT: Toby loves all animals

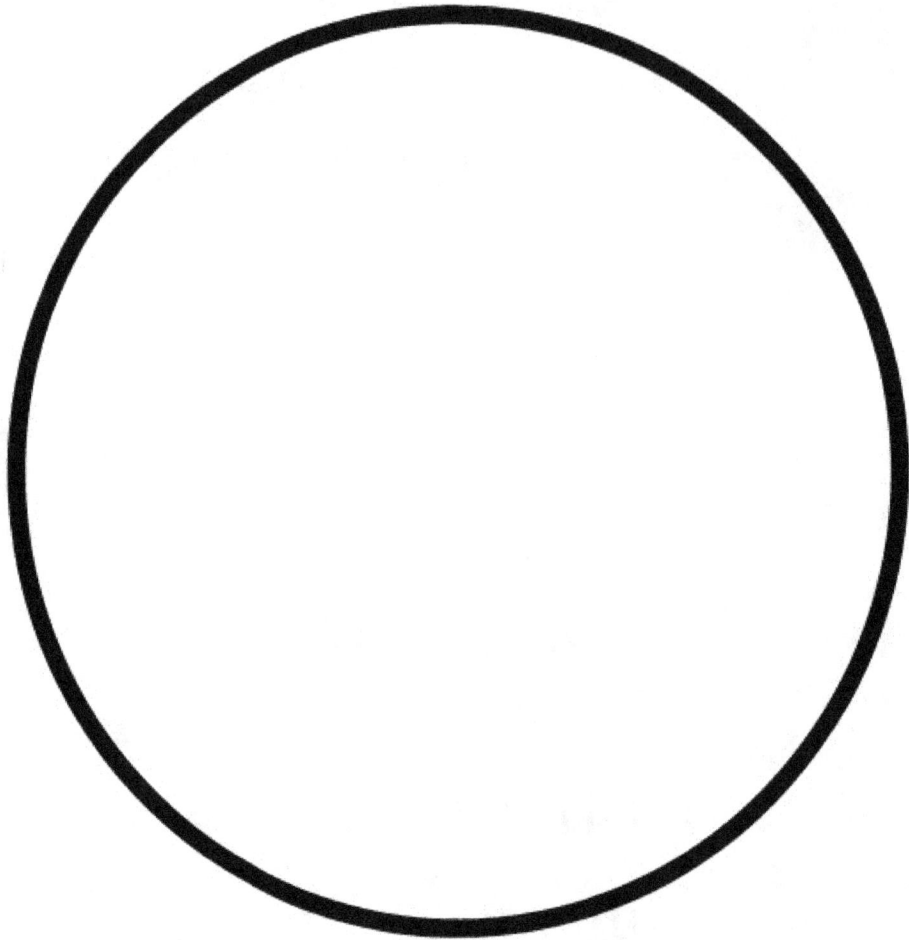

NAME: _____

BIRTHDAY: _____

FAVORITE ANIMAL: _____

FAVORITE COLOR: _____

FUN FACT: _____

_____

_____

Completely me

All four columns, rows, and boxes must have a triangle, a square, a circle and a heart. Complete the picture Sudoku.

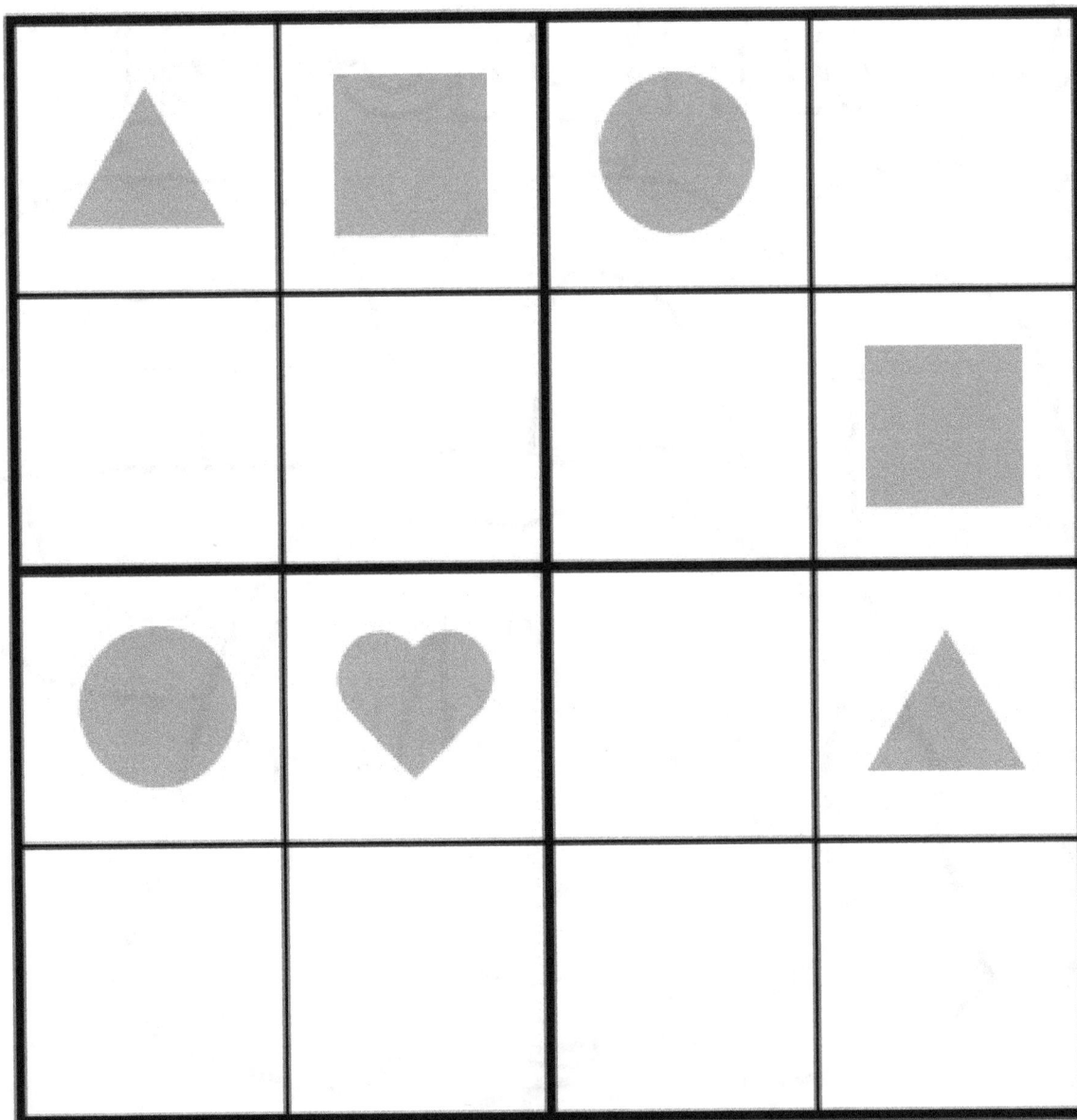

Can you match the "Completely Me" characters to their shadows?

1.

.a

2.

.b

3.

.c

4.

.d

All four columns, rows, and boxes must have a triangle, a square, a circle and a heart.
Complete the picture Sudoku.

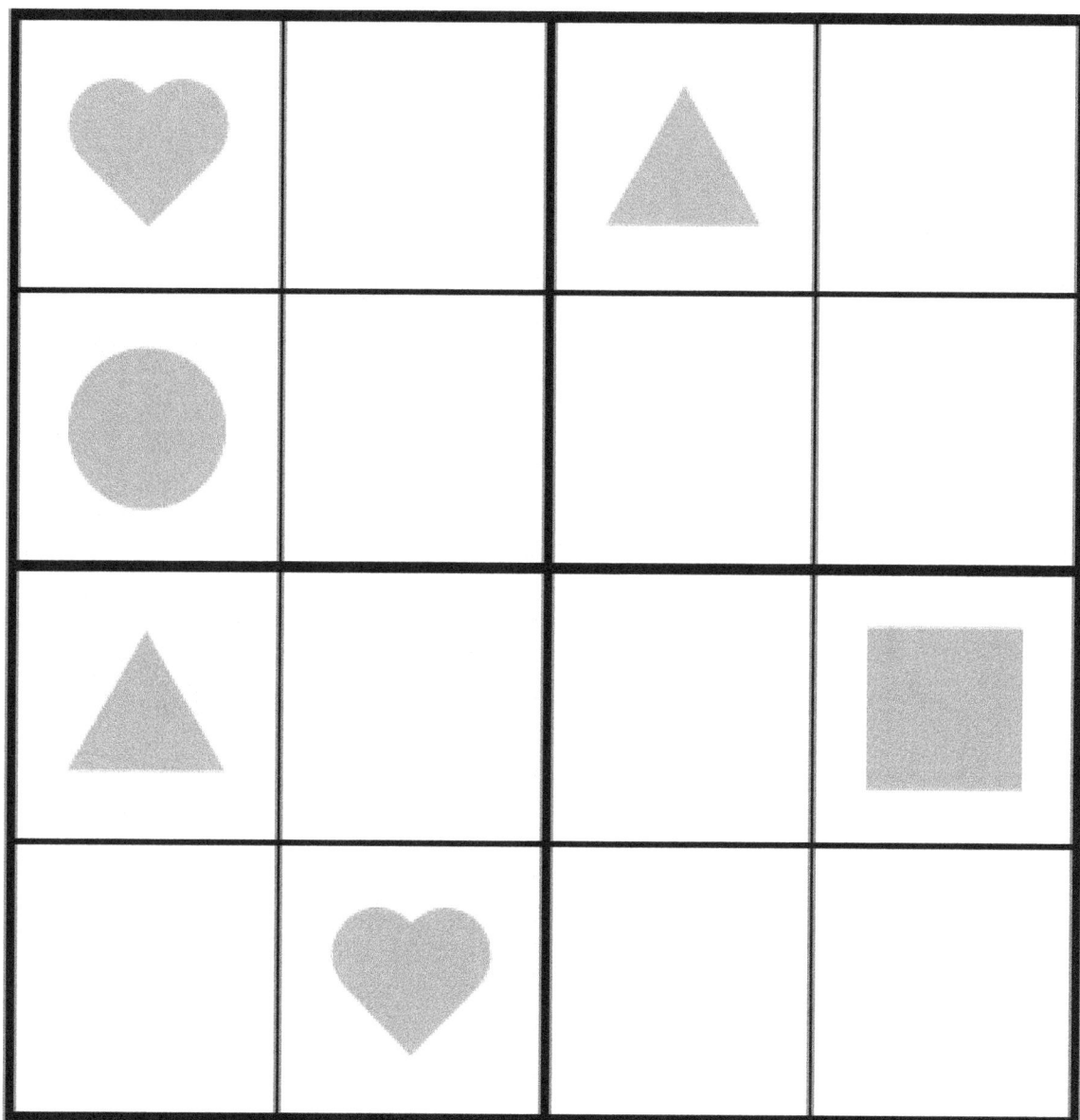

Tic Tac Toe.

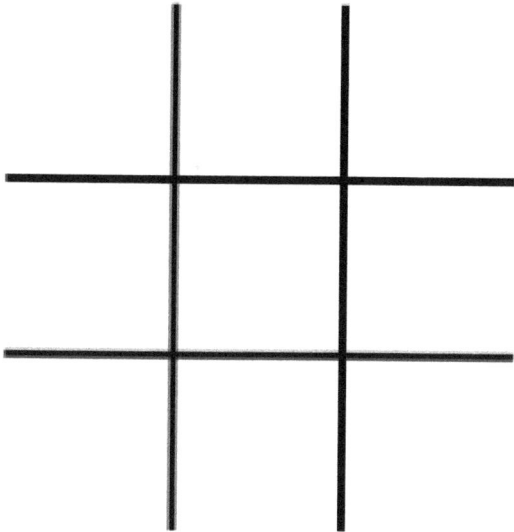
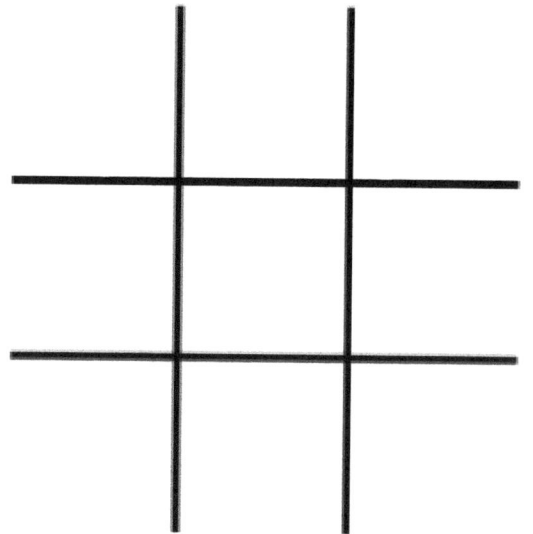

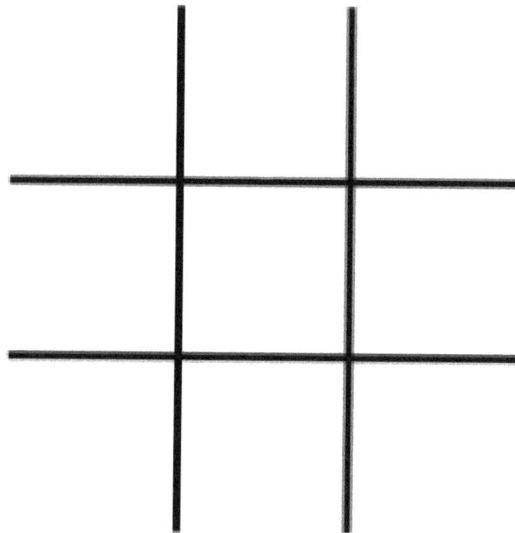

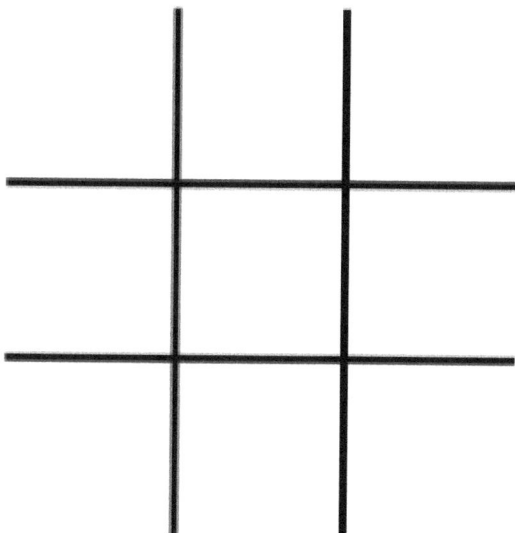
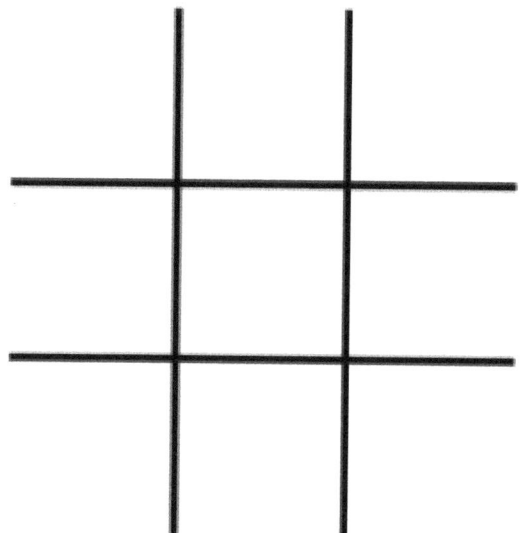

Tic Tac Toe.

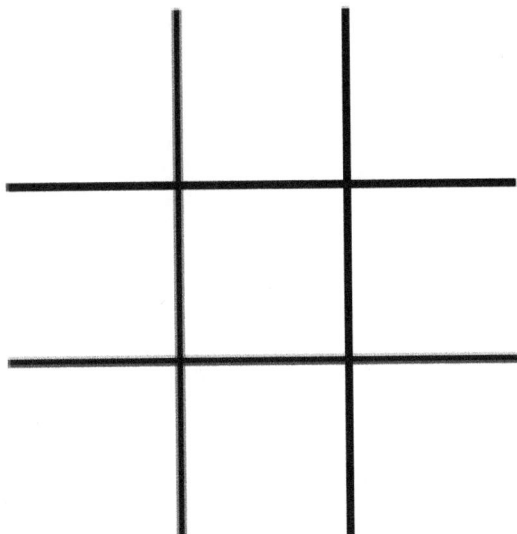 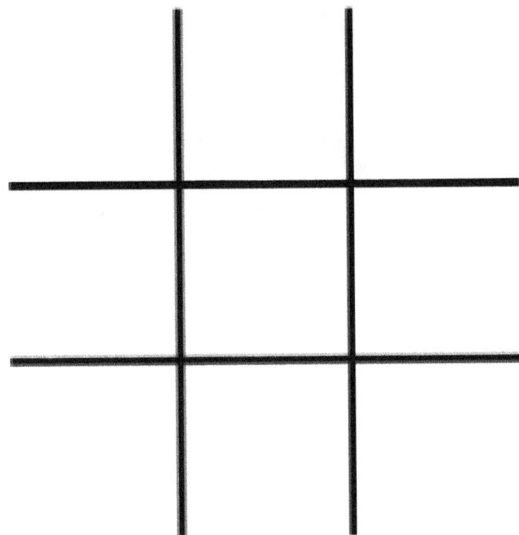

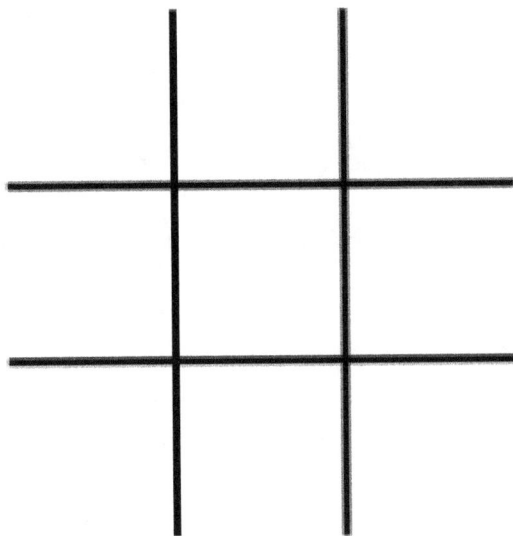

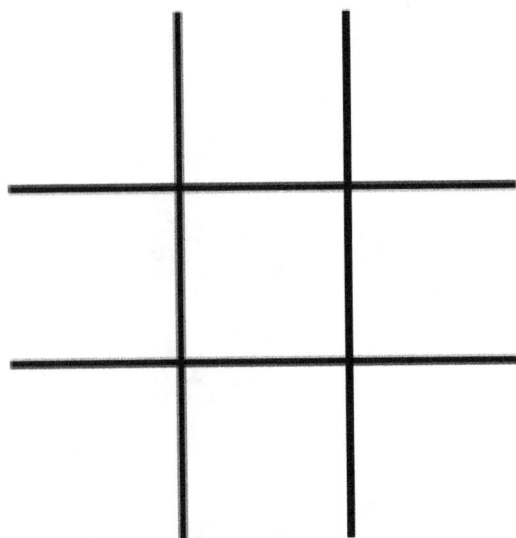 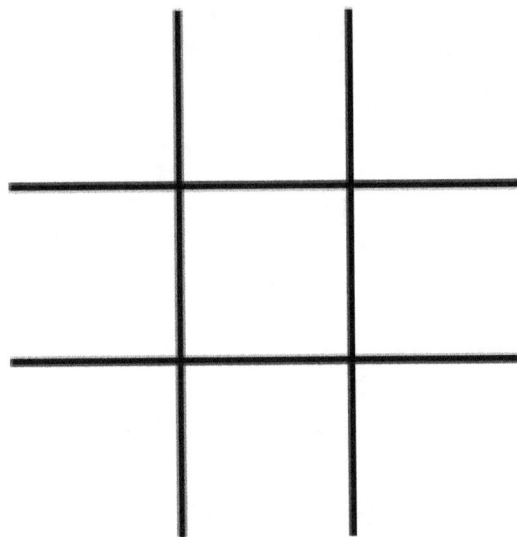

Complete the crossword puzzle.

All four columns, rows, and boxes must have a triangle, a square, a circle and a heart.
Complete the picture Sudoku.

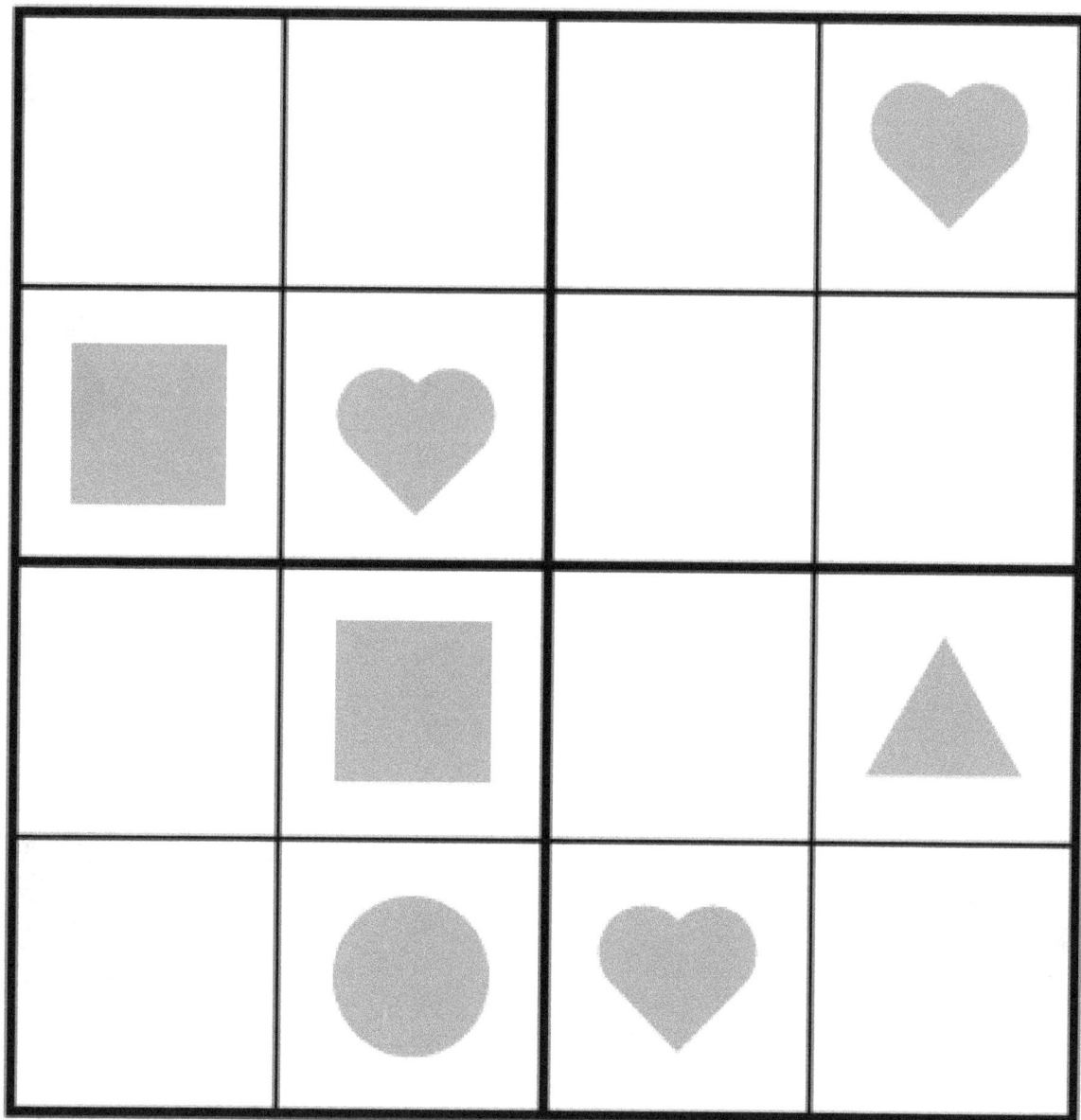

Can you match the "Completely Me" animals to their shadows?

 1.

 .a

 2.

 .b

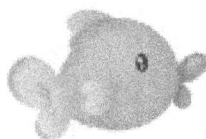 3.

 .c

 4.

 .d

 5.

 .e

Can you spot the 12 differences in these two pictures?

Connect the dots.

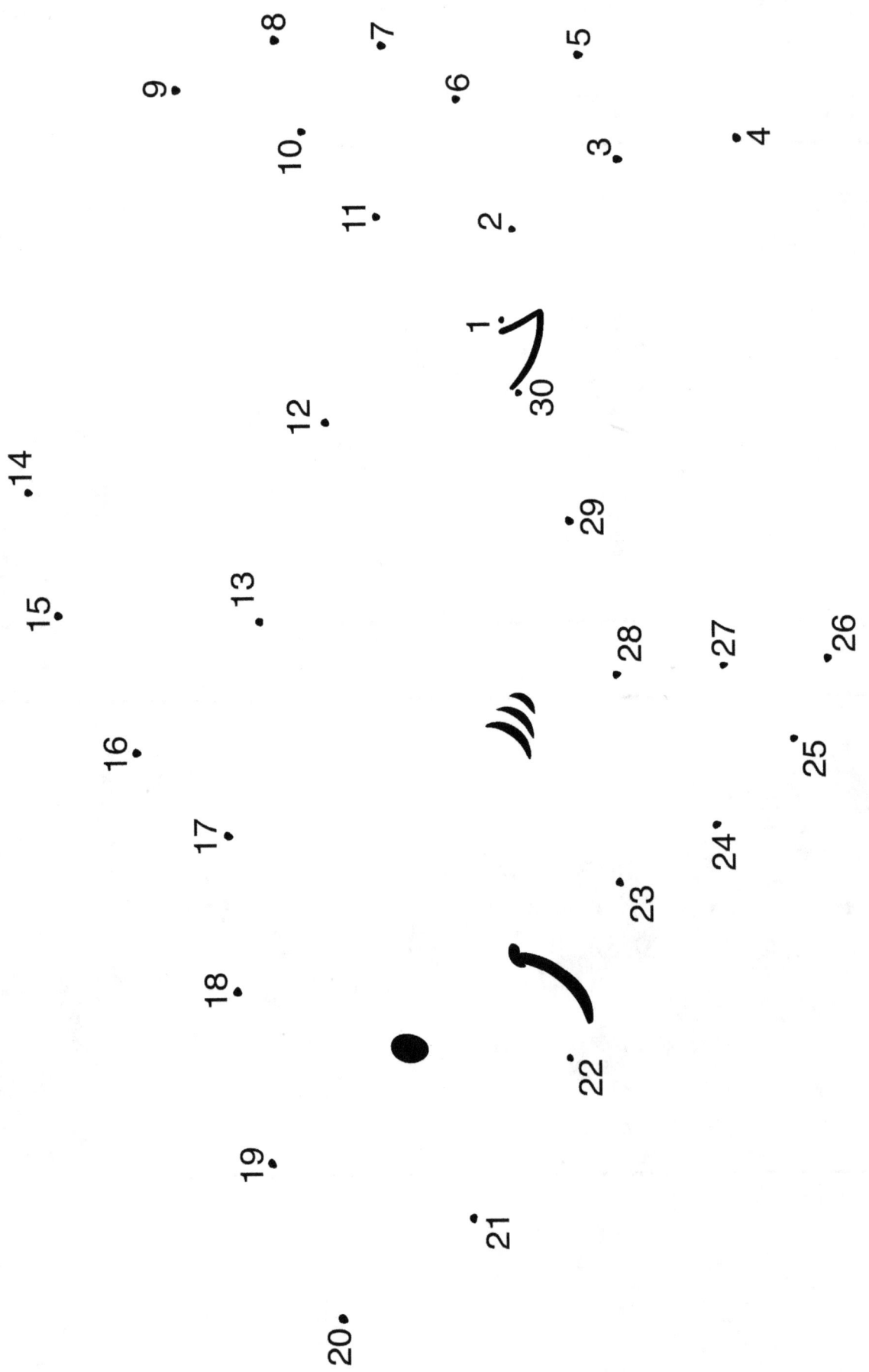

•8
•7
•5
9•
•6
10•
3•
•4
11•
2•
1
•30
12•
•14
29•
13•
15•
28•
•27
16•
25•
•26
17•
24•
18•
23•
19•
22•
21•
20•

All four columns, rows, and boxes must have a triangle, a square, a circle and a heart.
Complete the picture Sudoku.

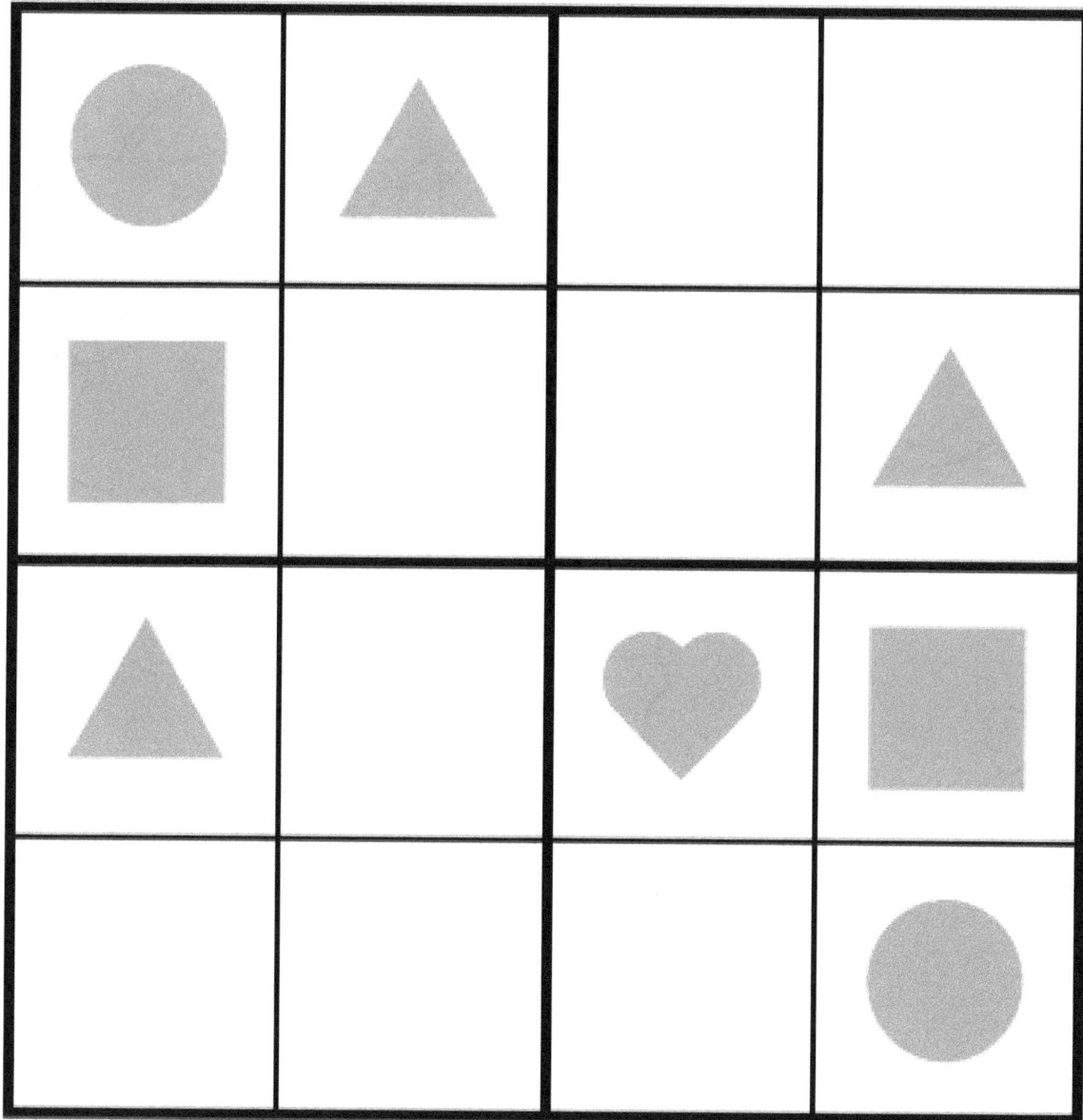

Can you help Matt find his fire truck toy?

START

Color by numbers.

1 - dark blue   2 - light blue   3 - green   4 - yellow   5 - red

All four columns, rows, and boxes must have a triangle, a square, a circle and a heart. Complete the picture Sudoku.

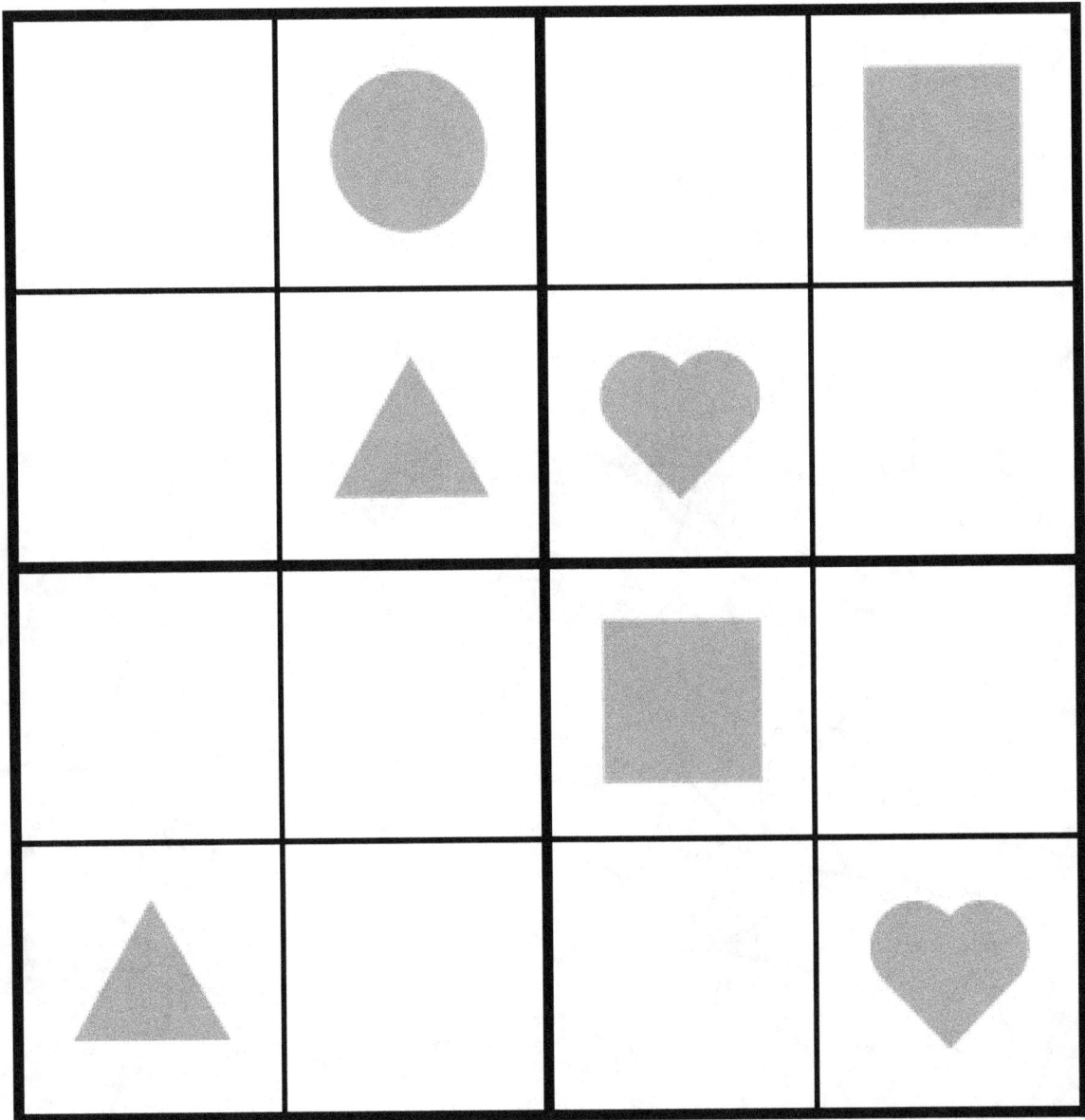

Complete the sequence by drawing the correct picture in the box.

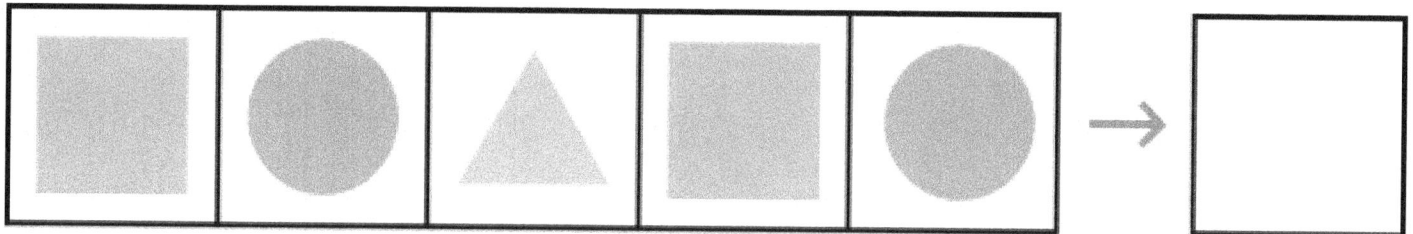

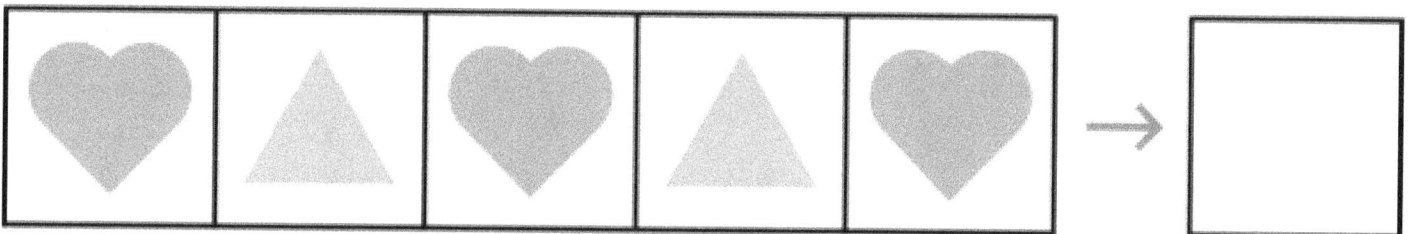

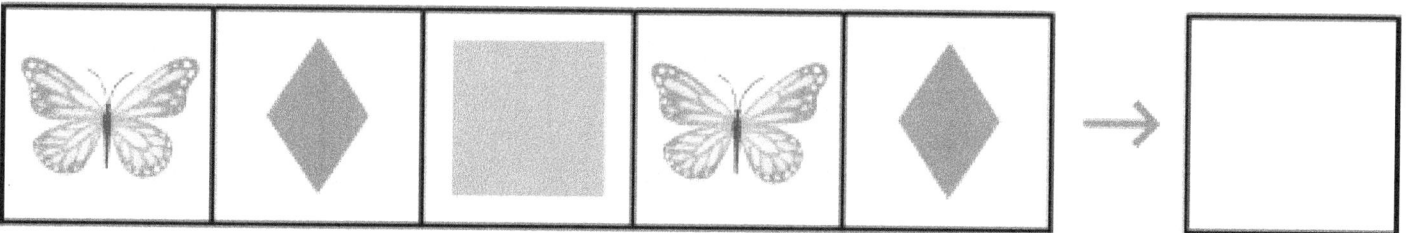

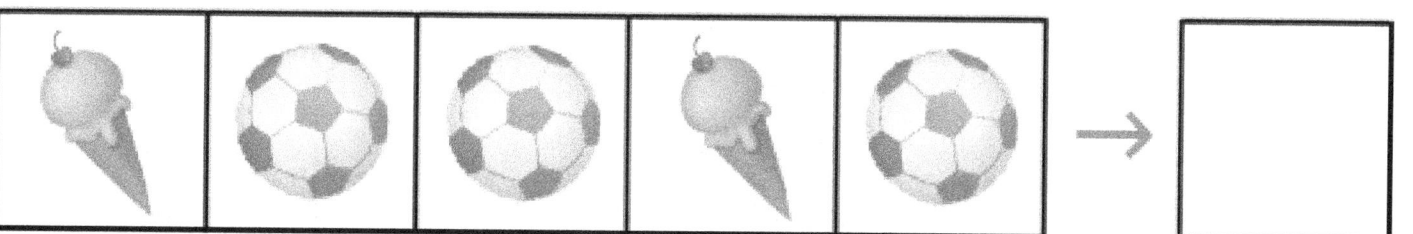

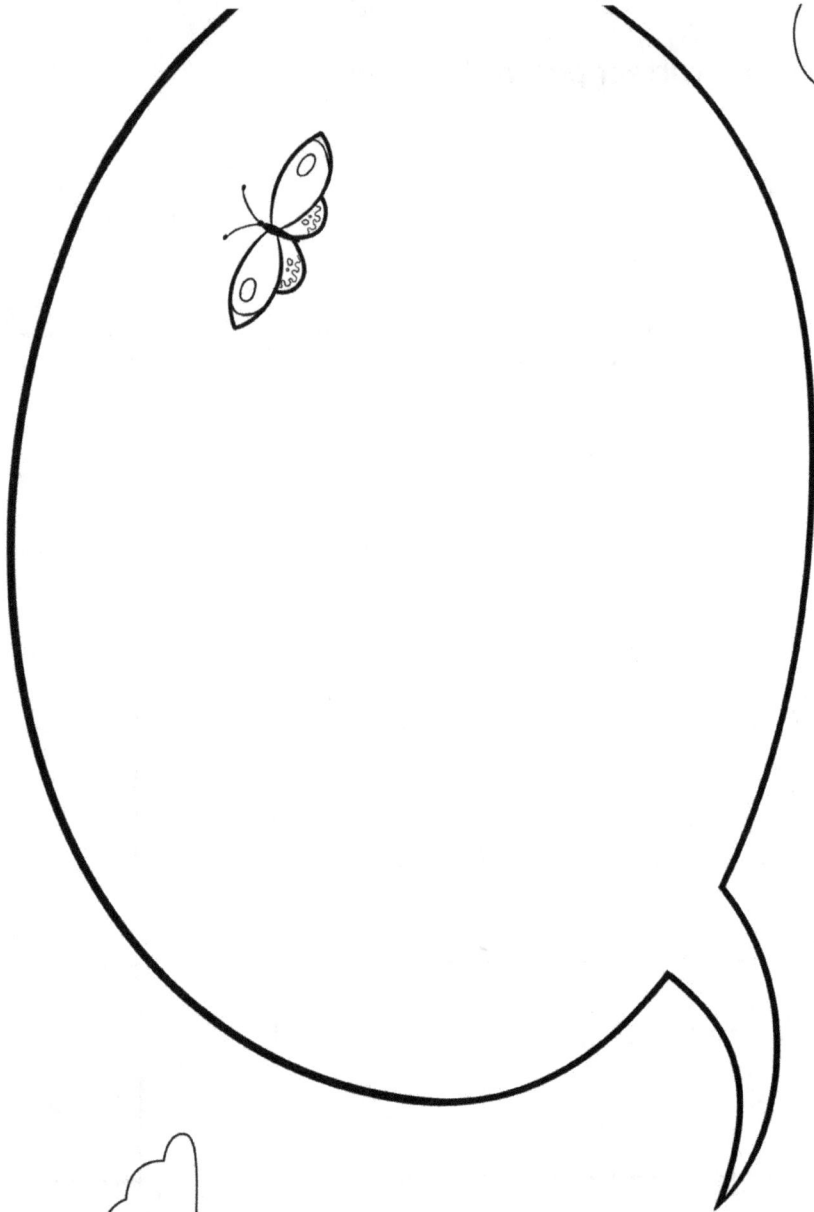

Word Search

S	Q	L	C	F	R	I	E	N	D	V
O	J	O	X	U	R	A	X	N	I	B
G	B	V	R	N	T	V	D	A	X	U
E	H	E	L	P	L	A	Y	J	P	T
C	A	I	Q	S	E	F	V	U	A	T
S	P	E	C	I	A	L	H	S	Z	E
F	P	I	C	K	R	U	Q	T	O	R
Z	Y	D	A	L	N	R	V	I	X	F
A	J	E	H	P	D	T	G	N	K	L
N	C	O	M	P	L	E	T	E	L	Y
T	X	B	E	S	P	A	R	K	L	E

- ☐ ANT
- ☐ BUTTERFLY
- ☐ COMPLETELY
- ☐ FRIEND
- ☐ FUN
- ☐ HAPPY
- ☐ JUSTINE
- ☐ LEARN
- ☐ LOVE
- ☐ PLAY
- ☐ SPARKLE
- ☐ SPECIAL

Connect the dots.

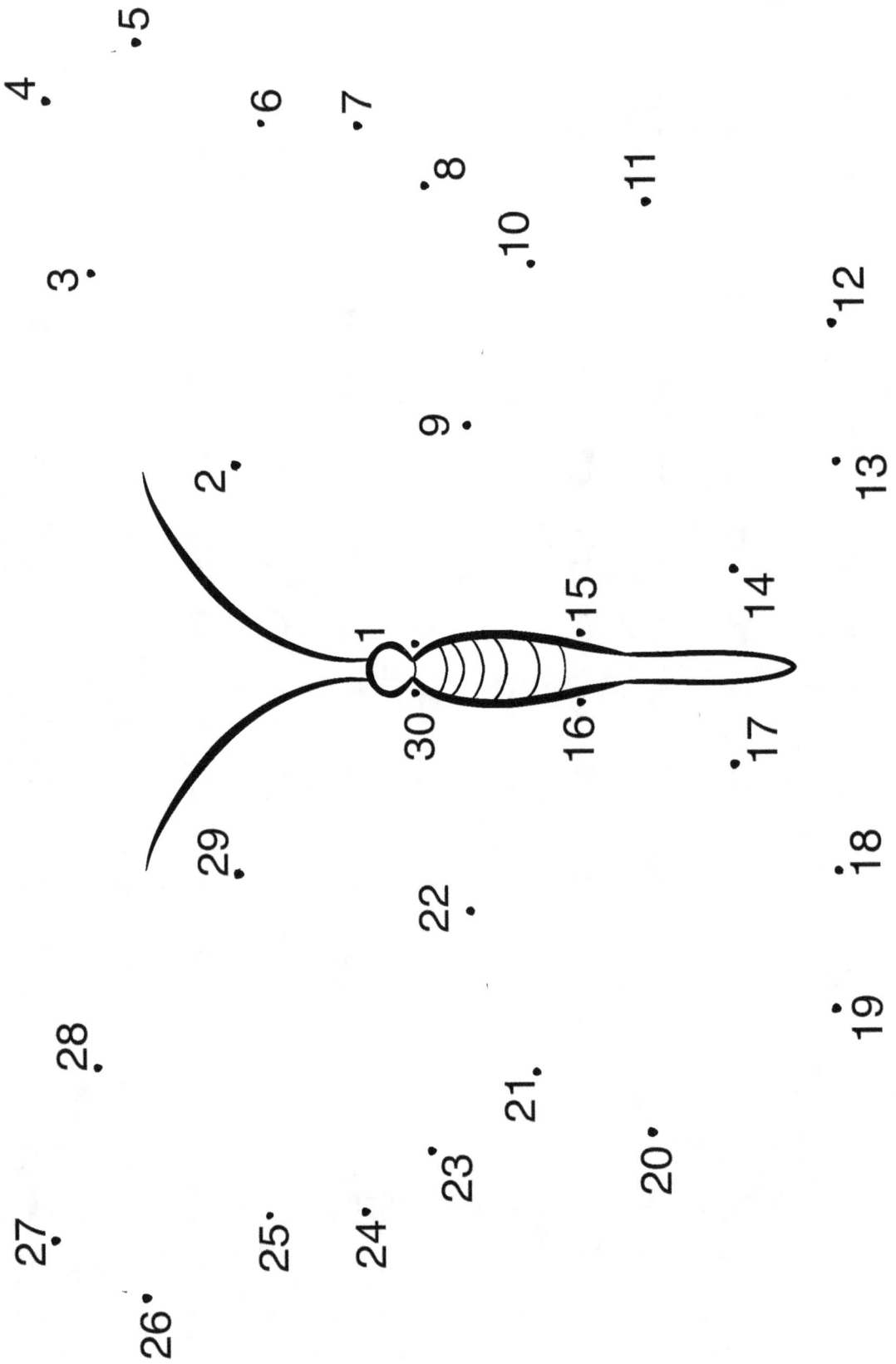

4

•5

3 •

•6

•7

•8

•10

•11

9 •

•12

2 •

•13

•15

•14

1

30•

16•

•17

29 •

18•

22 •

19•

28
•

21•

23•

20•

27•

25•

24•

26•

All six columns, rows, and boxes must have the numbers 1-6.
Complete the picture Sudoku puzzle.

6		4		2	
	1		3	4		6
	1		3		4
4		6		1	
	6		2		5
2		5	6		1

What is Matt painting? Draw on his canvas.

Can you help Justine find her book?

START

Use the boxes to copy the turtle drawing below.

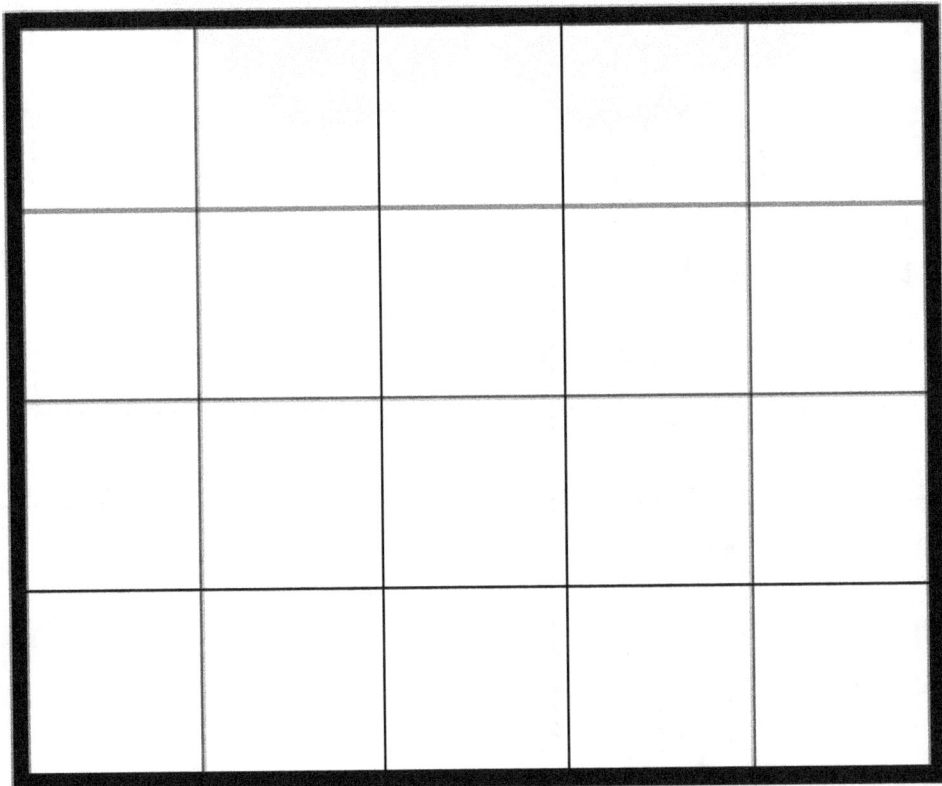

Complete the crossword puzzle. The black boxes indicate a space.

Decorate the butterfly wings.

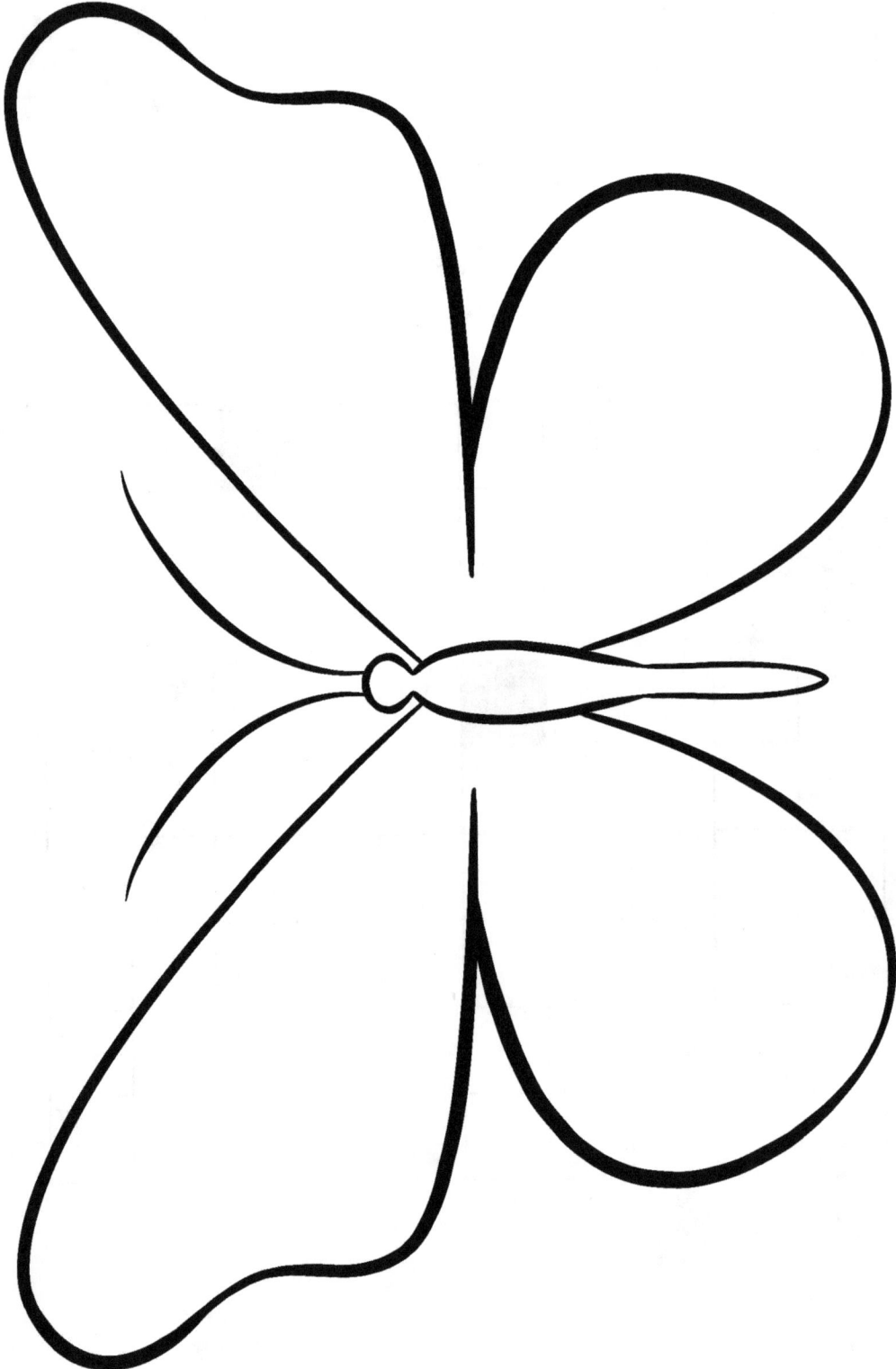

All six columns, rows, and boxes must have the numbers 1-6.
Complete the picture Sudoku puzzle.

5		2		4	
		3	5		6
2		4			5
6			4		
		5	3		
	1			5	

Can you match the "Completely Me" butterflies to their shadows?

 1.

 .a

 2.

 .b

 3.

 .c

 4.

 .d

 5.

 .e

 6.

 .f

 7.

 .g

 8.

 .h

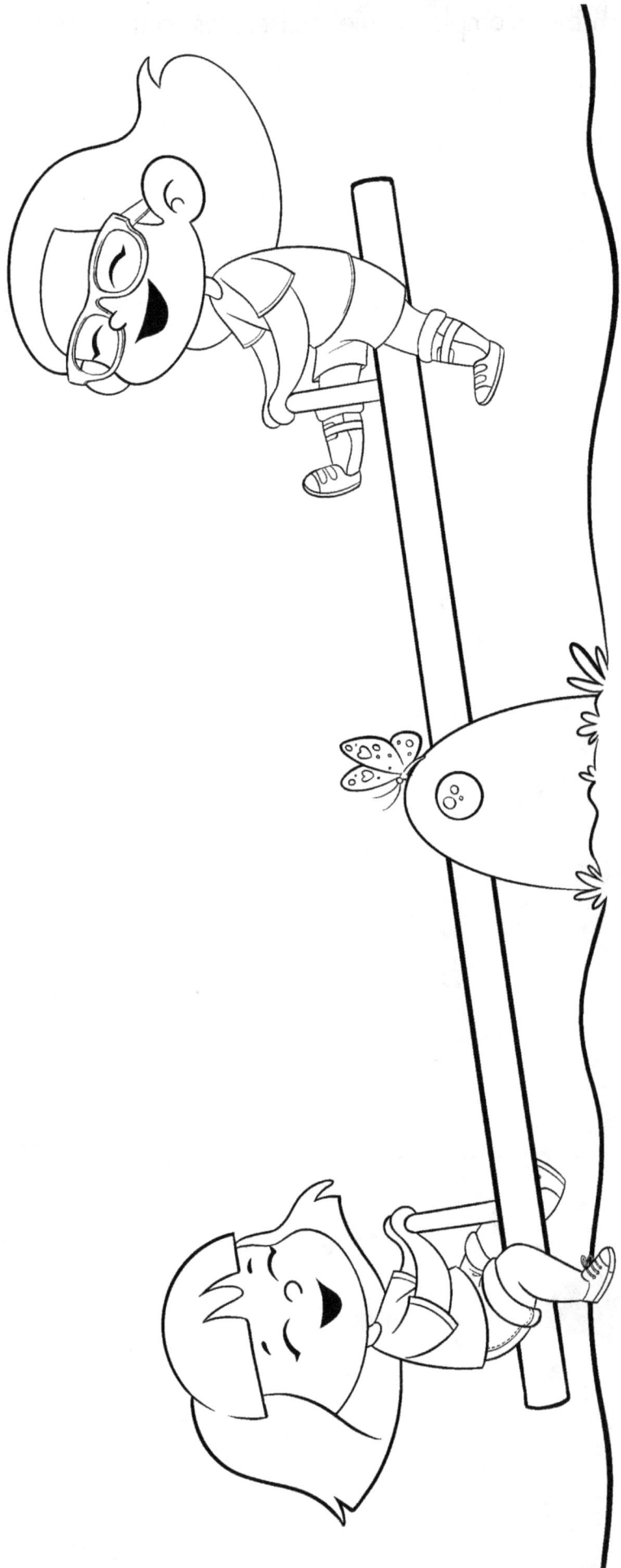

Can you spot the 10 differences in these two pictures?

All six columns, rows, and boxes must have the numbers 1-6.
Complete the picture Sudoku puzzle.

5	6	1			
	3		6		5
1		6			
	5				6
3		5		6	
			3		2

Draw a really fun hat for Matt.

Please write to me!

Dr. Justine Green
5900 Broken Sound Pkwy NW
Boca Raton, FL 33487

Dear Dr. Justine Green,

_____

_____

_____

_____

_____

_____

_____

_____

(your name and return address so I can write you back)

Answer Key:

16

38

5

8

14

17

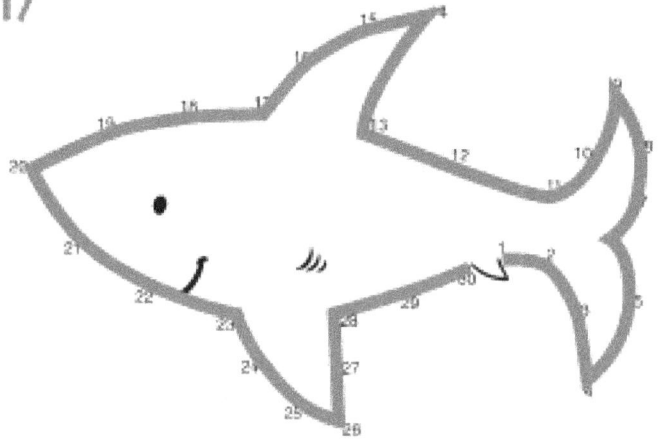

18

20

46

23

24
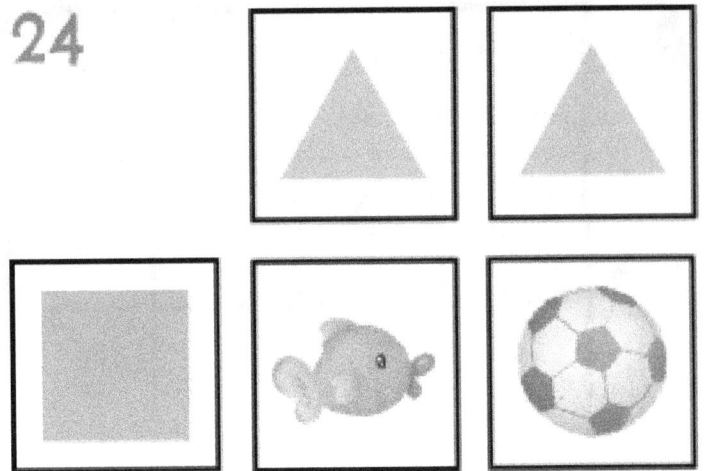

26
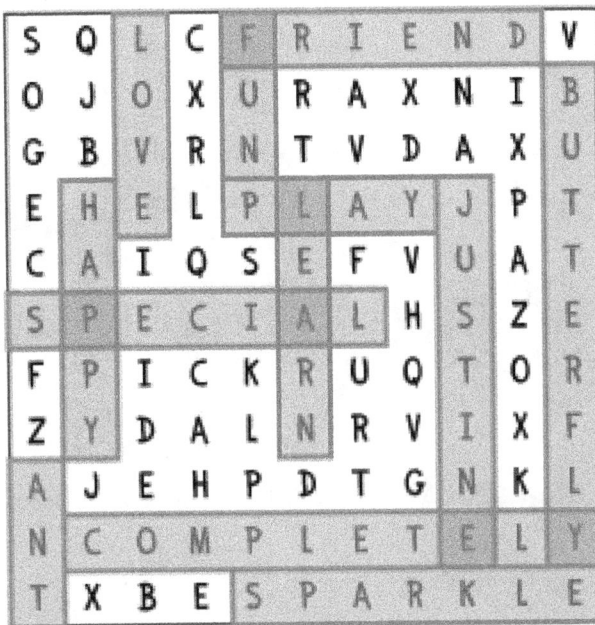

27
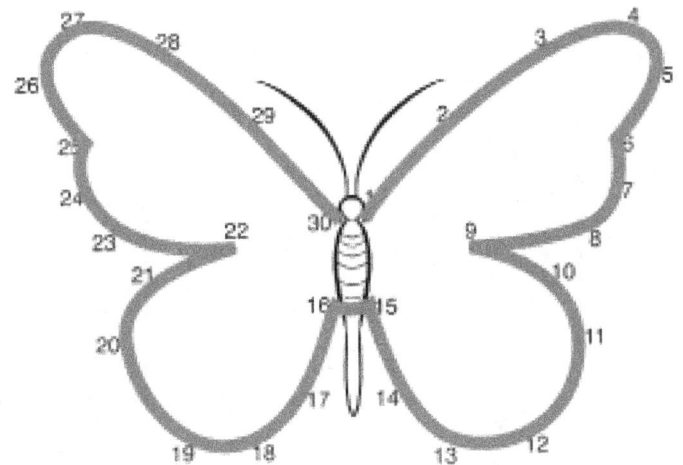

28
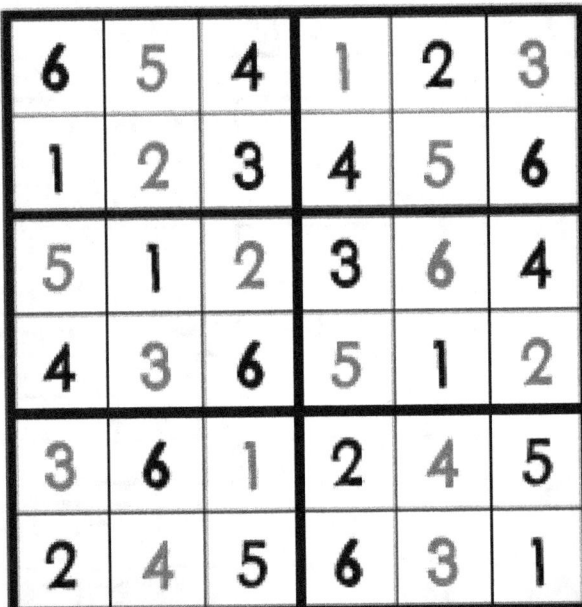

30

36

5	6	2	1	4	3
1	4	3	5	2	6
2	3	4	6	1	5
6	5	1	4	3	2
4	2	5	3	6	1
3	1	6	2	5	4

42

5	6	1	2	3	4
4	3	2	6	1	5
1	4	6	5	2	3
2	5	3	1	4	6
3	2	5	4	6	1
6	1	4	3	5	2

14

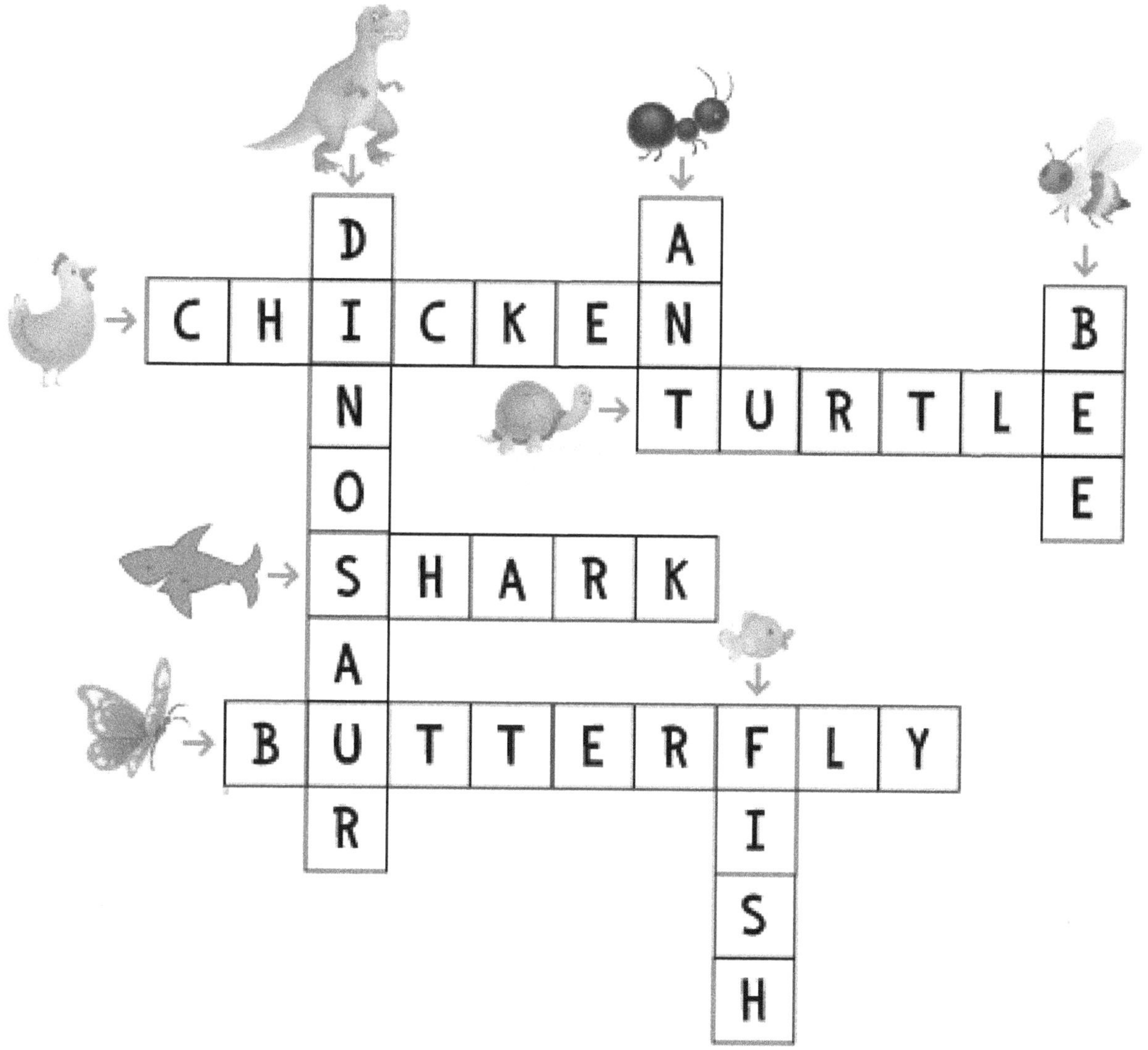
DINOSAUR
ANT
BEE
CHICKEN
TURTLE
SHARK
BUTTERFLY
FISH

```
        F
      F I R E     C R E A M
        R
  B     E                 B   B
  O ███████            A   R
C O N T R O L L E R   B R U S H
  K     U              L   U
        C              L   S
C L O C K                  H
```

FIRE
ICE CREAM
BOOK
CONTROLLER
FIRETRUCK
BALL
BRUSH
CLOCK

8

1. .d
2. .c
3. .a
4. .b

17

1. .c
2. .a
3. .e
4. .b
5. .d

38

1. .g   5. .b
2. .a   6. .h
3. .f   7. .c
4. .e   8. .d

www.ingramcontent.com/pod-product-compliance
Lightning Source LLC
Chambersburg PA
CBHW081639040426
42449CB00014B/3375